For my father, John A. Grohoske, who grew up on a farm, loved the land
and its creatures, and gifted me with that love—M. G. E.

To my mom, dad, and sister for guiding and inspiring me every day—N. G.

Text copyright © 2015 by Marilyn Grohoske Evans
Illustrations copyright © 2015 by Nicole Gsell
All rights reserved, including the right of reproduction in
whole or in part in any form. Charlesbridge and colophon
are registered trademarks of Charlesbridge Publishing, Inc.

Published by Charlesbridge
85 Main Street, Watertown, MA 02472
(617) 926-0329 • www.charlesbridge.com

Illustrations done in watercolor on Arches cold-press paper,
    and collaged digitally
Display type set in Hank BT by Bitstream
Text type set in Humper by Typotheticals
Color separations by Colourscan Print Co Pte Ltd, Singapore
Printed by 1010 Printing International Limited in Huizhou, Guangdong, China
Production supervision by Brian G. Walker
Designed by Whitney Leader-Picone

Library of Congress Cataloging-in-Publication Data
Grohoske Evans, Marilyn.
    Spit and sticks: a chimney full of swifts/Marilyn Grohoske Evans;
illustrated by Nicole Gsell.
        pages cm
    ISBN 978-1-58089-588-0 (reinforced for library use)
    ISBN 978-1-60734-770-5 (ebook)
    ISBN 978-1-60734-769-9 (ebook pdf)
1. Chimney swift—Juvenile literature. I. Gsell, Nicole, illustrator. II. Title.
III. Title: Chimney full of swifts.
QL696.A552G76 2015
598.7'62—dc23   2014010500

Printed in China
(hc) 10 9 8 7 6 5 4 3 2 1

Spit & Sticks

A Chimney Full of Swifts

Marilyn Grohoske Evans • *Illustrated by* Nicole Gsell

Charlesbridge

A stub-tailed, cigar-shaped bird streaks across the Texas spring sky. It's a chimney swift, thousands of miles from its other home in South America. The unusual little bird is thirsty. It spies a pond. Down it swoops. It skims the water for a drink. The bees and flies around the pond's edges scatter.

Now the swift soars high in the sky. What is it looking for? The farmer's chimney where it was born! Another swift hears its song and joins it. Now both swifts rock and roll, dip and dive, high in the sky.

Fun ends. Work begins. The birds' long claws snatch twigs
from the treetops. They carry them to the chimney in their beaks.
    Inside the chimney, the pair pastes the small sticks
together with a special glue made from their own sticky spit.
The pair won't quit until their half-saucer nest is perfect.

The nest is tested with one pure-white oval egg covered by a shiny, clear skin that hardens and becomes the shell. In one end of the egg is a pocket of air so the baby swift can breathe. Two more eggs are soon added to the nest. To keep the eggs warm, the birds snuggle close. They take turns fetching food.

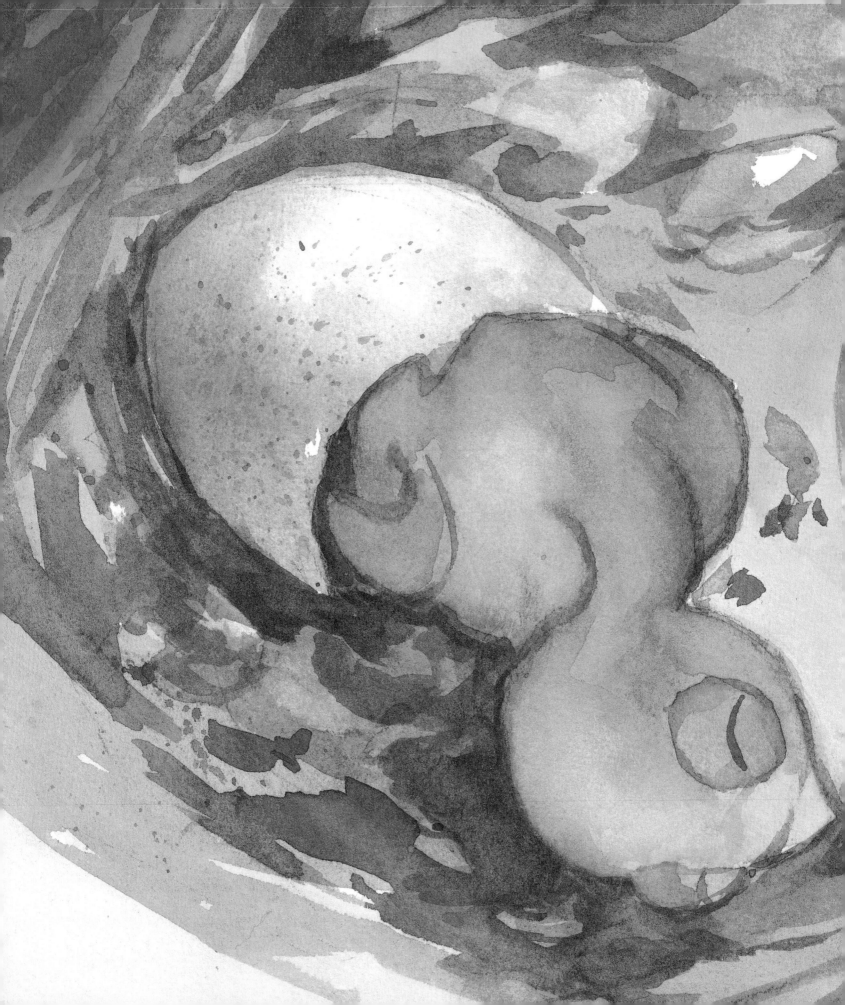

Three weeks pass. One sunny day, an egg wiggles. Through a tiny window, a baby's beak peeks out, then pecks and pecks—until out it tumbles, naked, pink, and wet.

Pip! The hatchling calls, trying to stand. But its spindly, short legs are weak. *Yip!* The baby calls again. More eggs break open. *Chip! Chip!* "Food!" their squawks say.

The adult swifts zip from the chimney. They cannot bring
the soggy fat flies and beetles for the babies fast enough.

The cornstalks in the farmer's field grow taller and stronger.
The young swifts grow bigger and braver. They push, shove, jab,
and jostle.

One day a brave young swift practices flapping its wings.
Suddenly the smallest swift tumbles from the wall! It
plummets through the darkness until . . .

. . . its strong feet and claws seize the edge of a brick. It sits on its sturdy, stiff tail feathers. Then it becomes a tiny helicopter, flying around inside the chimney.

After a moment, up it goes. It passes the nest, passes the other swifts. *Chip! Chip!* The other fledglings quickly follow until they reach the top of the chimney—the launchpad. The bravest lifts off first.

Summer heat swallows Texas. Chittering, the fledglings jubilantly feast and frolic, consuming tons of insects.

Days grow colder. Gusty winds soon strip the trees of their leaves and pound the pond's flying insects. The feathered family finds food scarce. Is it time to seek warmer land?

A rooster crows. Daylight dawns. A low rumble rouses every creature. Lightning flashes. The birds swarm into the sky. It is time.

Scritch. Scratch. Chip! Whoosh! The swift family swarms from the chimney. Higher and higher the little birds go. They joyously ride the wind as they join other swifts to become a black blur in the early-winter sky. They are headed for their other home.

And once again the chimney is silent . . . until next year.

About Chimney Swifts

Chimney swifts migrate from the Amazon region of South America to the United States and Canada, where they stay from late March until early November. They used to nest and roost in hollow trees, but when people moved west in the 1800s, they eliminated trees and built houses. The little birds, which used to be called American swifts, adapted by using chimneys to nest (like the one on the farm where the author's father, John A. Grohoske, grew up). Humans gave them a new name: chimney swift. The species is declining—down by more than half in the United States since 1970 and down by 95 percent in Canada. In the United States, they are protected by state wildlife codes and by federal law under the Migratory Bird Treaty Act of 1918.

Chimney swifts cannot perch or walk upright. Their strong feet tipped with four hook-like claws and stiff spines on their tail feathers help them cling to vertical surfaces. They spend most of their time in the air, where they fly and glide at twenty to thirty miles per hour from dawn until dusk.

Chimney swifts' sounds abound: Adults gently chipper inside their roost at night and when building their nest. Hatchlings erupt into a boisterous, explosive chattering if an adult enters the nest. If frightened, the hatchlings make a raspy sound, like a mechanical windup toy. At night young birds may sing—a sweet, soft, rhythmic peeping.

On average, adult chimney swifts are five inches long and weigh twenty-two grams (about the same as twenty-two paper clips). Males and females are the same size and color. Do an internet image search for "chimney swift" to see hundreds of photographs.

Chimney swifts gather in large groups at the end of the winter to return to South America. Do an internet image search for "chimney swift migration" to see a map of where they live and migrate.

What You Can Do
Read!

Educate your friends, your school, and your family. If you live in the chimney swifts' nesting area and your house has a masonry or clay flue-tile chimney, ask your parents to keep the top open and the damper closed from March through October to provide chimney swifts with a safe nesting site.

React!

Make sure your town knows how vital old silos and grain elevators are as nesting and roosting places for chimney swifts. Download an informational handout that includes how to construct a chimney swift nesting tower at www.chimneyswifts.org.

Recruit!

Gather friends and locate a roost in your area when hundreds and thousands of swifts gather before their fall migration. Count the number of chimney swifts that enter the roost. Visit www.chimneyswifts.org and click on "A Swift Night Out!" to access the reporting form or to see past reports.

Respect!

Remember that chimney swifts are wild animals. Don't touch a nest until after the birds have left for the winter, and then be sure to remove it before using the chimney, just as the family in the story does.